# Reflections on the Quran

## Mohammad Ahmad

Alreshah.net

Canada

**Alreshah**
**www.Alreshah.net**

If any error is found, please contact us through our website alreshah.net.

Book Layout © 2017 BookDesignTemplates.com

**Reflections on The Quran / Mohammad Ahmad**. -- 1st ed.
ISBN 978-1-9991711-1-7

# Contents

Introduction ...............................................................7

2:185 .......................................................................10

16:90 .......................................................................15

5:18 .........................................................................18

10:15-16 ..................................................................21

17:23-25 ..................................................................25

3:79-80 ....................................................................29

17:85 .......................................................................33

**18:54** ......................................................................35

7:33 .........................................................................39

**7:31** ........................................................................42

18:23-24 ..................................................................45

41:34-36 ..................................................................47

15:9 .........................................................................50

3:134 .......................................................................52

29:8 .........................................................................55

18:58 .......................................................................57

3:135 .......................................................................59

18:23-24.................................................61

15: 95 - 99...............................................65

29:2-6...................................................69

3:59-60..................................................72

49:6.....................................................75

7:28-29..................................................77

41:46....................................................81

5:83.....................................................83

16:90....................................................85

2:204-206................................................88

21:35....................................................91

49:13....................................................94

The End..................................................97

# CHAPTER 1

# Introduction

Since my childhood, my mother encouraged me to read the Quran from cover to cover during Ramadan. If I finished, I got Eidyah, which is a monetary gift given during Eid after Ramadan was over. Those memories are engraved in my memory; actually, I can remember that early exposure to the Quran from as soon as I could read, and its words had a huge impact on my personality.

There is a great deal of night activity during Ramadan, as most Muslims fast in the day. I remember I kept messing up on the pages I needed to cover per day in order to finish the Quran by the end of the month. So, by the 24th or 25th day of Ramadan, I started spending more time reading the Quran and tried to avoid watching cartoons on TV. As I grew up and learned more Arabic vocabulary, I could grasp a better understanding of the verses. Some of them really had an effect on me. I would stop and re-read them, thinking how well those verses were constructed and reflecting on the deep meanings they held.

Fast-forwarding, I saw one of the great scholars talking about how to benefit from Ramadan with the Quran, and he said, "Most Muslims read the Quran in Ramadan, and some read it cover to cover. But does reading change them? Do they gain more knowledge, or do they just read words?"

That was a changing point in my life, as I started to think about what that scholar had said. I then set a goal that in Ramadan, I would read one page and check every interpretation and explanation for those verses until I fully captured the meaning. That changed my pace from reading cover to cover in 29 days to finishing a few pages in 29 days. But those few pages had the most significant benefits to my Islamic knowledge.

This year I decided to do something different: to collect verses and think about them and explain them, reflecting on the current time. By doing that, I share the knowledge I gain with all readers. I am not claiming that I am a scholar nor an expert in Tafseer (explaining the Quran), but I am knowledge seeker who enjoys thinking about the verses of the Holy Quran, and linking it to our current time based on the words, meaning, and knowledge gained from Tafseer. I started this book on the first day of Ramadan 2019 and stopped on the last day of it, hoping it would benefit the reader and inshallah, will follow it with another book next year.

In this book, a chapter is a cross-reference to Surat. If a chapter title is 1:1, that means the first verse is from Surat Al Fatah. Then I follow it by the verse in Arabic for reference, then the direct translation of the verse is between quotation marks followed by my interpretation and views in a standard font. I hope you enjoy this light book, and I pray to Allah to forgive any mistake or error.

# 2:185

شَهْرُ رَمَضَانَ الَّذِي أُنزِلَ فِيهِ الْقُرْآنُ هُدًى لِلنَّاسِ وَبَيِّنَاتٍ مِّنَ الْهُدَىٰ وَالْفُرْقَانِ فَمَن
شَهِدَ مِنكُمُ الشَّهْرَ فَلْيَصُمْهُ وَمَن كَانَ مَرِيضًا أَوْ عَلَىٰ سَفَرٍ فَعِدَّةٌ مِّنْ أَيَّامٍ أُخَرَ يُرِيدُ اللَّهُ
بِكُمُ الْيُسْرَ وَلَا يُرِيدُ بِكُمُ الْعُسْرَ وَلِتُكْمِلُوا الْعِدَّةَ وَلِتُكَبِّرُوا اللَّهَ عَلَىٰ مَا هَدَاكُمْ وَلَعَلَّكُمْ تَشْكُرُونَ

" *The month of Ramadan [is that] in which was revealed the*
*Qur'an.* "

- Quran's first verses were revealed in Ramadan before
fasting even became a must, and even before Mohammad was
ordered to spread the religion of Islam, the first verse of Quran
was revealed to Mohammad PBUH (Peace Be Upon Him) when
he was away from Makkah in one of its mountains meditating.
That shows how important this month is to Muslims beyond

fasting, and it is a link to the Quran, as many Muslims do read it cover to cover in the month of Ramadan .

*"A guidance for the people and clear proofs of guidance and criterion. "*

- This a description of the Quran as guidance for all people, an international religion without borders that doesn't favor one race over another. It is a religion to guide people based on clear statements without error. The highest authority where things are judged to; the Quran says what is true and what is false. If laws are in the Quran, they are the best humans can have as laws. It is a system based on an understanding of human nature and is a middle ground between the extremism of limitations and extremism of lack of social responsibility.

*"So, whoever sights [the new moon of] the month, let him fast it. "*

- here the order to fast Ramadan which starts from the 2nd year after the prophet Migrated to Madinah, and also another point many ask about, which is how the Islamic calendar is calculated; it is based on the lunar cycle, which follows the moon phases, so there are either 29 or 30 days in the month, depending on the moon sighting.

*"and whoever is ill or on a journey - then an equal number of other days."*

- Here where Islam's understanding of different people's needs and issues plays a role, conditioning the general order that every sane adult Muslim should follow, as the aim of religion is to protect life, and fasting might harm certain people. So, it is not recommended to fast if a person is sick. Another example of something forbidden being allowed is if a person is stuck in a place where there is no food or water, and he finds a dead wild pig (which would normally be forbidden to eat), due to the need of survival, he is allowed to have as much as needed to provide him with enough energy to sustain his life.

*"Allah intends for you ease and does not intend for you hardship and [wants] for you to complete the period "*

- Worshiping Allah is a way of ease and happiness in life. Fasting might sound challenging, but it is ultimately beneficial when it is done the right way, not only to one's health but also in terms of touching the soul and uplifting the spirit. It is also an important reminder of many people in this world who do not have access to food and water, increasing awareness and compassion towards those in need worldwide.

*"and to glorify Allah for that [to] which He has guided you, and perhaps you will be grateful. (185)"*

- This verse praising Allah for his Guidance is linked by scholars to Takbeer (praising Allah in collectively in mass ) in the Eid days after Ramadan, as Muslims praise Allah in their Eid prayers, thanking him for the health they have which allows them to fast, and for his blessings on them.

# CHAPTER 3

# 16:90

إنَّ الله يَأْمُرُ بِالْعَدْلِ وَالْإِحْسَانِ وَإِيتَاءِ ذِي الْقُرْبَىٰ وَيَنْهَىٰ عَنِ الْفَحْشَاءِ وَالْمُنكَرِ وَالْبَغْيِ يَعِظُكُمْ لَعَلَّكُمْ تَذَكَّرُونَ

*"Indeed, Allah orders justice and good conduct and giving to relatives."*

- A clear order from Allah to be just to others and to self, to not harm others nor harm self, and to be just when talking about Allah, refraining from making false claims about him or linking false idols to him. Justice, when dealing with people, includes using fairness and not cheating and lying. And he orders "Ihasan," which is the highest level of good conduct, when the outside action is good but not as good as the intentions, which were limited by circumstances outside of the person's control. "Ihasan" is a pure intention and pure heart.

The mention of "giving to relatives" means whether they are close as cousins or further removed; helping relatives is a way to build a strong society and strong community based on love, wishing good to others and removing envy. This part includes every good action a person can think about. For example, if a teacher works hard with the aim of reaching perfection in the task of teaching kids, with the intention that what is done is done for God, they are rewarded for that good deed.

*"and forbids immorality and bad conduct and oppression. "*

- this part includes every action Islam sees as a sin, even actions that seem good from the outside, but the intentions in the heart are bad. Also, Allah forbids oppression, regardless of whether it is taking people's money by force or by trickery, or if it is terrorism, mass murder, rape, or any crimes that involve severe harm to others. Those are huge sins that Allah the Almighty forbids, and they are given severe punishments in life and afterlife, as they go beyond personal sin where no one else is involved. When others are harmed, they have their right to forgive or not. That is why those sins are seen as the worst in Islam because forgiveness includes a third party. So even if a person asks God for forgiveness, it is linked to the forgiveness of the harmed person, which will be a huge challenge to obtain on judgment day.

*"He admonishes you that perhaps you will be reminded "*

- Allah Almighty reminds us to follow the orders in the Quran to have happiness in this life and beyond and to avoid what he forbids, as it will cause only harm to us or others in this life                                    and                                    beyond.

# 5 : 18

وَقَالَتِ الْيَهُودُ وَالنَّصَارَى نَحْنُ أَبْنَاءُ اللّـهِ وَأَحِبَّاؤُهُ  قُلْ فَلِمَ يُعَذِّبُكُم بِذُنُوبِكُم  بَلْ أَنتُم بَشَرٌ مِّمَّنْ خَلَقَ  يَغْفِرُ لِمَن يَشَاءُ وَيُعَذِّبُ مَن يَشَاءُ  وَلِلّـهِ مُلْكُ السَّمَاوَاتِ وَالْأَرْضِ وَمَا بَيْنَهُمَا  وَإِلَيْهِ الْمَصِيرُ

*" But the Jews and the Christians say, "We are the children of Allah and His beloved."*

- Both claim that they are beloved by God. Jews claim that God has chosen and favors them, and Christians claim that they are children of God and are his beloved and that Jesus is the son of God or God himself, depending on which denomination a person follows.

*"Then why does He punish you for your sins?"*

- Then why are you worried about his punishment, and why do you have different views about Jesus PBUH and even about God? A Jew for a Christian is an unbeliever and sinner, and a Christian for a Jew is polytheistic and a sinner because of the claim of the Trinity?

*"Rather, you are human beings from among those He has created"*

- Your group of mankind doesn't elevate yourselves beyond what you are; you both go back to Adam as the first human for Jews, Christians, and also Muslims. You are the same as any human; there is no difference in front of God, nor is a group favored because of race. Race doesn't have value for God, as all people trace back to the first human. And you as mankind are one of many species God created; some we know of and many we don't. God knows better what he created, so there is not any reason to elevate yourself.

*" He forgives whom He wills, and He punishes whom He wills."*

- He is Almighty the Just he forgives to whom he wants and punishes whom he wants. We are equal in front of him regardless if you are a Jew or grandson of Mohammad PBUH. We will be judged equally based on what we have done and what we believed in. Our race is not a privilege to give us any kind of benefit.

*" And to Allah belongs the dominion of the heavens and the earth and whatever is between them, and to Him is the [final] destination. "*

- This a reminder that mankind is a tiny part of his creation, so don't go beyond your limits and claim about Allah what is not related to him. Don't claim you are his children nor claim he had a son or he is more than one, or he needs someone to be associated with him. Remember that to him, you will return. He is              the              final              destination.

# CHAPTER 5

# 10:15-16

وَإِذَا تُتْلَىٰ عَلَيْهِمْ آيَاتُنَا بَيِّنَاتٍ ۙ قَالَ الَّذِينَ لَا يَرْجُونَ لِقَاءَنَا ائْتِ بِقُرْآنٍ غَيْرِ هَٰذَا أَوْ بَدِّلْهُ ۚ قُلْ مَا يَكُونُ لِي أَنْ أُبَدِّلَهُ مِن تِلْقَاءِ نَفْسِي ۖ إِنْ أَتَّبِعُ إِلَّا مَا يُوحَىٰ إِلَيَّ ۖ إِنِّي أَخَافُ إِنْ عَصَيْتُ رَبِّي عَذَابَ يَوْمٍ عَظِيمٍ

قُل لَّوْ شَاءَ اللَّـهُ مَا تَلَوْتُهُ عَلَيْكُمْ وَلَا أَدْرَاكُم بِهِ ۖ فَقَدْ لَبِثْتُ فِيكُمْ عُمُرًا مِّن قَبْلِهِ ۚ أَفَلَا تَعْقِلُونَ

*" And when Our verses are recited to them as clear evidence, those who do not expect the meeting with Us say, "Bring us a Qur'an other than this or change it."*

- The same things told to Mohammad PBUH 1400 years ago are said to many Muslims today, such as, "It is an old book," or " It doesn't fit the new world" or "Why don't you change it or reform it as other religions have done," or "Why insist on holding on to this old text?." The same claims are made all these years later because humans have the same basic ideas and tendency to change laws to fit their own desires or twist words based on situations they are in, trying to entertain their current needs

*" Say, [O Muhammad], "It is not for me to change it on my own accord. I only follow what is revealed to me. Indeed, I fear if I should disobey my Lord, the punishment of a tremendous Day."*

- Here Mohammad PBUH stated clearly, and every Muslim believing in the divinity of the Quran does state, it is not about us or our views and desires. It is God's words, and we have a responsibility to say what Allah revealed without a change or twist. And we fear great punishment if we twist even a letter. We as Muslims are the Guardians of Allah's book, just as Mohammad PBUH was in his time. And those laws are the orders of a wise and knowledgeable God. His wisdom and knowledge are beyond all of mankind's abilities combined. When he establishes laws, he knows what is coming, what was before, and what is now, so to claim we know better or that his words need to be updated is against the basic principle of monotheism. By saying it needs change, we claim we know better than God, and that is a claim no way a person believing in a wise and just God can make.

*"If Allah had willed, I would not have recited it to you, nor would He have made it known to you, for I had remained among you a lifetime before it. Then will you not reason?"*

- Where are their minds? They knew Mohammad PBUH since childhood; he didn't read or write; he didn't even recite poetry. He reached his 40s before becoming a prophet, and the prophecy was not his choice; it is Allah's will. He recites the Quran as it is revealed to him and teaches it to people because he is the prophet by the will of Allah. So, don't approach him to change the Quran, as it is not in his hands.

# CHAPTER 6

# 17:23-25

Allah says in his holy book in Surat Al-Asra:

وَقَضَىٰ رَبُّكَ أَلَّا تَعْبُدُوا إِلَّا إِيَّاهُ وَبِالْوَالِدَيْنِ إِحْسَانًا ۚ إِمَّا يَبْلُغَنَّ عِندَكَ الْكِبَرَ أَحَدُهُمَا أَوْ كِلَاهُمَا فَلَا تَقُل لَّهُمَا أُفٍّ وَلَا تَنْهَرْهُمَا وَقُل لَّهُمَا قَوْلًا كَرِيمًا (23) وَاخْفِضْ لَهُمَا جَنَاحَ الذُّلِّ مِنَ الرَّحْمَةِ وَقُل رَّبِّ ارْحَمْهُمَا كَمَا رَبَّيَانِي صَغِيرًا (24) رَبُّكُمْ أَعْلَمُ بِمَا فِي نُفُوسِكُمْ ۚ إِن تَكُونُوا صَالِحِينَ فَإِنَّهُ كَانَ لِلْأَوَّابِينَ غَفُورًا (25)

*"And your Lord has decreed that you not worship except Him, and to parents, good treatment. Whether one or both of them reach old age [while] with you, say not to them [so much as], "uff," and do not repel them but speak to them a noble word."*

- We are ordered to worship only him and disregard every claim of association with him or other claims linked to the

Almighty. The Almighty clearly shows how important the rights of parents are in Islam. There are many Hadith in Sunnah about how a person should treat his own parents. Especially if they took good care of him, gave him the best education, and fed him well, when they are of an old age where they are in need and can't help themselves, the person should look after his parents and provide them with what they need, as they did for him when he was in need.

*" And lower to them the wing of humility out of mercy "*

- This is an example of an analogy used in the Quran, where a human in his 30s to 40s is usually in his peak of strength and is well established. His wings are spread like a flying bird, but his parents might be in a weak state and in need of mercy. They may need help in some cases when they can't clean themselves and need their kids to do that to preserve their dignity. So, the person shows humility to them as a sign of love and mercy.

*" and say, "My Lord, have mercy upon them as they brought me up [when I was] small."*

- That moment of showing kindness is the best time to ask God for a favor, and even that favor should be asked for the parents. Treating one's parents is so important that God elevates this deed to a level close to where monotheism is. When the prophet PBUH was asked about the biggest sin, he said, "The biggest of Al-Ka`ba'ir (the great sins) are (1) to join others as partners in worship with Allah, (2) to murder a human being, (3) to be undutiful to one's parents and (4) to make a false statement or give false witness ( Al Bukhari )."

# 3:79-80

مَا كَانَ لِبَشَرٍ أَن يُؤْتِيَهُ اللَّـهُ الْكِتَابَ وَالْحُكْمَ وَالنُّبُوَّةَ ثُمَّ يَقُولَ لِلنَّاسِ كُونُوا عِبَادًا لِّي مِن دُونِ اللَّـهِ وَلَـٰكِن كُونُوا رَبَّانِيِّينَ بِمَا كُنتُمْ تُعَلِّمُونَ الْكِتَابَ وَبِمَا كُنتُمْ تَدْرُسُونَ (٧٩) وَلَا يَأْمُرَكُمْ أَن تَتَّخِذُوا الْمَلَائِكَةَ وَالنَّبِيِّينَ أَرْبَابًا ۗ أَيَأْمُرُكُم بِالْكُفْرِ بَعْدَ إِذْ أَنتُم مُّسْلِمُونَ

*" It is not for a human [prophet] that Allah should give him the Scripture and authority and prophethood and then he would say to the people, "Be servants to me rather than Allah,"*

- That response is to anyone claiming that any prophet called himself divine or link himself to God as partner or son. It is illogical that God will send a prophet and select a person, teach him and reveal to him a book, and teach him wisdom. And then that guide starts calling people to worship himself! That claim itself is against the monotheism of God where God is all-knowing and above mistake and error.

*"but [instead, he would say], "Be pious scholars of the Lord because of what you have taught of the Scripture and because of what you have studied."*

- Taught people the religion, and what is better than submission to one God, doing great deeds, asking people to do great deeds, avoiding immorality, avoiding sin, and being helpful and supportive. Be an example for others to follow.

*"Nor could he order you to take the angels and prophets as lords. Would he order you to disbelief after you had been Muslims?"*

- Why should he send prophets to ask you to associate themselves with the Almighty? Why should he order them to move people from disbelief or polytheism to another type or style of the same? That itself is illogical and makes no use of the prophecy. But the truth he sent with his prophets to guide and give the knowledge to be Muslims ( submission to Allah) by free will.

# CHAPTER 8

# 17:85

وَيَسْأَلُونَكَ عَنِ الرُّوحِ ۖ قُلِ الرُّوحُ مِنْ أَمْرِ رَبِّي وَمَا أُوتِيتُم مِّنَ الْعِلْمِ إِلاَّ قَلِيلاً

*" And they ask you, [O Muhammad], about the soul."*

- A group of people asked Mohammad PBUH what the soul is. The Soul is something God created. It is the difference between a dead body and a living person. It is something we can't define, but we can't reject or ignore.

*"The soul is of the affair of my Lord."*

- That soul is a creature by God; he created it and knows how it acts and what will happen to it. Mohammad PBUH only teaches what God taught him and told him; he doesn't form his own views or ideas. He is a messenger delivering the message he was given.

*"And mankind have not been given of knowledge except a little."*

- How far we reach in knowledge and how much more we will know and master as science is not very much. Most of our understanding is using what God created and learning the application over time, but regardless of how far we go in knowledge, it is still seen as little. We don't even know everything about our own body and how to find a cure for it when we get sick.

# CHAPTER 9

# 18:54

God says in his holy book:

وَلَقَدْ صَرَّفْنَا فِي هَذَا الْقُرْآن لِلنَّاس مِن كُلّ مَثَلٍ  وَكَانَ الْإِنسَانُ أَكْثَرَ شَيْءٍ جَدَلاً

" And We have certainly diversified in this Qur'an for the people from every [kind of] example; "

- Every kind of example and method of how to worship God in the right way, the way he ordered, without a change or modification, and at the same time, correcting the changes in previous religions based on the aims of their clergy or social elite. The Quran includes a response to false claims about Allah, a clear monotheistic way and path to worship the Almighty in the way he wants, for all people, without a difference or discrimination, worship by heart, words, and actions. A book includes laws to manage human relations with other humans , with society, and with the environment without forgetting to focus on the person's own self, a balanced approach between the extremism of thoughts and ideologies— a middle path. That verse also confirms the relevance of the Quran to fit every time and place, regardless of whether it is the 7th century or the 27th century.

*" but man has ever been, most of anything, [prone to] dispute. "*

- That is a fact they argued with Mohammad PBUH and before him argued with Jesus PBUH and all the prophet before PBUT ( Peace be upon them) , and today is something people still argue. There is a difference between debating, which is a natural result of seeking knowledge and arguing for the sake of arguing. When a person is asked to provide evidence to support a claim, that person starts a chain of arguments, avoiding a clear answer, or using evidence which is not related to the subject discussed, or twisting it to fit a narrative.

The verse also can be seen as an order to avoid this kind of discussion that has no benefits and exists just to feed someone's ego. That is why Muslims when they note someone arguing without a base, should protect themselves from being pulled into that, and simply leave the discussion after a clear statement of the facts. Or they might ask for clear evidence.

# 7:33

Allah say in his holy book:

قُلْ إِنَّمَا حَرَّمَ رَبِّيَ الْفَوَاحِشَ مَا ظَهَرَ مِنْهَا وَمَا بَطَنَ وَالْإِثْمَ وَالْبَغْيَ بِغَيْرِ الْحَقِّ وَأَن تُشْرِكُوا بِاللهِ مَا لَمْ يُنَزِّلْ بِهِ سُلْطَانًا وَأَن تَقُولُوا عَلَى اللهِ مَا لاَ تَعْلَمُونَ

" *Say, "My Lord has only forbidden immoralities - what is apparent of them and what is concealed -* "

- This verse starts with "say" as statement and order to Mohammad PBUH to state clearly what God forbids. God forbids immoralities, whether they are done out in public where everyone can see or are hidden in a closed room or behind a social media screen. Or they could even be immoralities hidden in the heart, like envy or pride.

" *and sins*"

- Any action God forbids in the Quran and in Sunnah, or not following God orders, or actions are forbidden based on the rules of the Quran and Sunnah.

*" and oppression without right"*

- Oppression against people by taking their rights can be seen as stealing or hidden actions such as planning a trap or tricking a person into a bad deal, or hiding information which might save or benefit them. This action is a sin too, but it is mentioned separately to emphasize that even taking the rights of others—which some might not see as sin—is forbidden in Islam. The idea of stepping on others to reach my goal is not welcomed in Islam.

*" and that you associate with Allah that for which He has not sent down authority, "*

- To claim that a person, regardless if he is a prophet or not, is associated with God or can help after his death or can see and hear the calls of people. Those are all things only Allah can do, and there is no one who can help beside him.

*" and that you say about Allah that which you do not know."*


- This part is linked to the previous one. A false claim about Allah is disbelief in monotheism, as is claiming he had a son, or he is one of many, or claiming the Almighty lacks ability or knowledge. There are many claims that we hear today without any link to the truth. They just simply don't know .

# CHAPTER 11

# 7:31

يَا بَنِي آدَمَ خُذُوا زِينَتَكُمْ عِندَ كُلّ مَسْجِدٍ وَكُلُوا وَاشْرَبُوا وَلاَ تُسْرِفُوا ۚ إِنَّهُ لاَ يُحِبُّ الْمُسْرِفِينَ

*" O children of Adam, take your adornment at every masjid,"*

- Muslims should make sure that when they go to pray, they are in their best clothes and have their best hygiene. It is a habit in many places for Muslims to put their best perfumes on when they go to pray because they are standing in front of Allah, the king of kings. That respect should be reflected in the personal choice of clothing and cleanliness. Being clean is an important part of Islam, and maintaining that cleanliness is essential. It can be seen in many aspects of Islam. For example, before a person prays, they need to perform Wudu (an action of cleaning and washing a part of the body).

*" and eat and drink, but be not excessive. Indeed, He likes not those who commit excess."*

- From this verse, they are many benefits :

1. Don't overeat, even if it is halal food and halal drink, as this can cause harm. Today many of us have an issue with the scale, and many of us are overweight, and that excess is the reason. Does it do us any good? The list of sicknesses from obesity is almost unlimited, from high blood pressure to sleep issues.

2. It also reflects the Islamic belief that we are not the owners of the earth. We are accountable and responsible for it. I don't own the animals and should not just go on killing and abusing. We should only eat what we need to, not hunt for fun or destroy the land for fun. Our biggest problem is that many humans feel an entitlement to take ownership of the whole earth!!!

3. Allah doesn't like excess, even if it is halal. Excess can even be seen in religion when a person ignores his family's needs and spends time worshipping without

caring, or claims things are forbidden, assuming he worships Allah better or makes new prayers not known before. Allah dislikes such actions.

# 18:23-24

وَلاَ تَقُولَنَّ لِشَيْءٍ إِنِّي فَاعِلٌ ذَلِكَ غَدًا (٢٣) إلاَّ أَن يَشَاءَ اللـهُ وَاذْكُر رَّبَّكَ إِذَا نَسِيتَ وَقُلْ عَسَىٰ أَن يَهْدِيَنِ رَبِّي لأَقْرَبَ مِنْ هَذَا رَشَدًا

" *And never say of anything, "Indeed, I will do that tomorrow," Except [when adding], "If Allah wills."*

- This order for every Muslim is that God's will is above a person's intention. Our actions and plans are based on our will, but the one whose will is above all is Allah. By saying that, we submit to Allah. That is why maybe the most common word you hear from Muslims is "inshallah," which means "if God wills."

If you get used to saying "inshallah" with every action, it becomes a habit. Sometimes, we may want to start a lousy thing, like maybe we wish to take revenge or start a fight. We may say, "Inshallah, tomorrow I will take my revenge" and then we may ask ourselves if the action we are planning tomorrow is what Allah asks of us, or if he asks us to forgive and have mercy. That itself is a reminder to every Muslim that intends to do a lousy action to check if his action is against Allah's order. The person feels ashamed of himself to include Allah's name in wrongdoing, which affects the person's intention to misbehave and might even make him stop.

*" And remember your Lord when you forget [it] and say, "Perhaps my Lord will guide me to what is nearer than this to right conduct."*

- Praise Allah and remind yourself that Allah's will is above all, and if he wants to save you, no one can harm nor take good from you. Pray to him to guide you to right conduct. Hold to the faith and follow his final religion.

# 41:34-36

Allah Almighty, says in his book

وَلَا تَسْتَوِي الْحَسَنَةُ وَلَا السَّيِّئَةُ ادْفَعْ بِالَّتِي هِيَ أَحْسَنُ فَإِذَا الَّذِي بَيْنَكَ وَبَيْنَهُ عَدَاوَةٌ كَأَنَّهُ وَلِيٌّ حَمِيمٌ (٣٤) وَمَا يُلَقَّاهَا إِلَّا الَّذِينَ صَبَرُوا وَمَا يُلَقَّاهَا إِلَّا ذُو حَظٍّ عَظِيمٍ (٣٥) وَإِمَّا يَنزَغَنَّكَ مِنَ الشَّيْطَانِ نَزْغٌ فَاسْتَعِذْ بِاللَّـهِ إِنَّهُ هُوَ السَّمِيعُ الْعَلِيمُ

*"And not equal are the good deed and the bad. "*

It is clear that good actions or deeds are not equal to the bad or evil ones, and this verse talks about deeds or actions against others.

*"Repel [evil] by that [deed] which is better; "*

If someone acts badly to you, such as an insult or lie about you, do good in return.

*"and thereupon the one whom between you and him is enmity [will become] as though he was a devoted friend. (34) "*

- And that will have an effect on people and will make some rethink and change their minds based on good deeds and being kind to them. Also, some people might act badly, not because they are bad, but because they had a bad day or maybe are ignorant. Especially today, with polarized media, many people might be fed false information and act based on the assumption that it is factual information.

*"But none is granted it except those who are patient, and none is granted it except one having a great portion [of good]. (35) "*

- Here the verse mentions that the ability to act good in response to bad deeds is hard and requires great patience. Sometimes the harm is so painful and so severe, it makes it hard to forgive and act with good deeds. One who can do this is a person with great ability, and God will reward that ability with a great portion of good, which is heaven.

*"And if there comes to you from Satan an evil suggestion, then seek refuge in Allah. Indeed, He is the Hearing, the Knowing. (36)"*

If Satan suggests to a person to take revenge on a person who did evil than that person should avoid those thoughts and seek refuge in Allah, so they can avoid the desire for revenge, even if that person returns the good with bad, Allah knows what is hidden in the hearts of people and hears what is talked about behind closed doors. He is the refuge of the believer, and the believer should not worry if depending on Allah.

# 15:9

إِنَّا نَحْنُ نَزَّلْنَا الذِّكْرَ وَإِنَّا لَهُ لَحَافِظُونَ

*"Indeed, it is we who sent down the Qur'an, and indeed, we will be its guardian. "*

The Almighty sent the Quran in verses to Mohammad PBUH over his prophecy, as the Quran was revealed in parts, as a final book from the Almighty, a book without error nor mistake, the word of God who knows what was, what is, and what will be tomorrow.

The Almighty will protect his book from change until the last day, and that is well seen, as there has been no change in the Quran since 1400, and there won't be any change. It is a book saved in the heart of Muslims, the only book which doesn't need to be in a physical book form to be saved. A Muslim's heart is the physical place it is saved in. Since Mohammad PBUH taught tens of thousands of his companions, the same Quran is repeated every day in every Mosque from south to north and east to west, around the globe, in one language. So what more than this protection has any book had?

Islam is an international religion, where it is sent to mankind without a doubt and is not limited by time, where other religions are time-period limited for a small group of people.

# 3:134

الَّذِينَ يُنفِقُونَ فِي السَّرَّاءِ وَالضَّرَّاءِ وَالْكَاظِمِينَ الْغَيْظَ وَالْعَافِينَ عَنِ النَّاسِ  وَاللَّـهُ يُحِبُّ الْمُحْسِنِينَ

*" Who spend [in the cause of Allah] during ease and hardship."*

- In this verse, Allah describes the behavior of righteous believers, who will give charity in comfortable times with their extra money, and also who give charity in hardship, and this might be more challenging. Many of us today see people in need, and even if we are in need, still give charity out for those in greater need.

*" and who restrain anger."*

- Another challenge is to hold your anger. Due to today's fast-paced world and self-centered societies, anger is the response to many situations. If someone serves your food order wrong, drives in front of you, or doesn't greet you, you get mad, and all of those can be purely unintentional mistakes! So what about instances where people intend to harm you or make you angry? Can you hold your anger then, and satisfy the verse requirement?

*" and who pardon the people "*

- It even pushes the bar higher, mentioning not only restraining the anger but also forgiving people. If someone did something to anger you, regardless of intention, forgiveness is a great deed, as it is hard on personal ego and self-pride to forgive someone who insults you.

*" and Allah loves the doers of good; "*

- and those action of charity and restrain anger, and forgiving people are good deed Allah loves, and love who so them as that person avoid harming other and control anger which might make him        do        more        sin        seeking        revenge.

# CHAPTER 16

# 29:8

وَوَصَّيْنَا الْإِنسَانَ بِوَالِدَيْهِ حُسْنًا  وَإِن جَاهَدَاكَ لِتُشْرِكَ بِي مَا لَيْسَ لَكَ بِهِ عِلْمٌ فَلَا
تُطِعْهُمَا  إِلَيَّ مَرْجِعُكُمْ فَأُنَبِّئُكُم بِمَا كُنتُمْ تَعْمَلُونَ

*" And We have enjoined upon man goodness to parents. "*

- Although the translation is Enjoined which mean order or instructed but the Arabic word is وصينا "wasena" and it can be translated better to trust, so Allah Almighty trusted human with good treatment to His parents and this trust would be checked against in the day of Judgement did person kept the trust in safe and protected by good treatment and care of his parent, or he broke it and treat them badly.

*" But if they endeavor to make you associate with Me that of which you have no knowledge, do not obey them. "*

- If they try hard to make follow their religion if they are not Muslims, or even if they are Muslims, and try hard to associate Allah with anything like a group Guru or such , don't follow them. God didn't say here, "don't visit them " or " don't help them." He just limits it to not following them, as Right of God is above every right, and Monotheism, which is believing in Allah without associating anything with him, is higher than following listen to parents' orders or talk, but at the same time, they still have the right to good treatment and kindness regardless of this position.

- *"To Me is your return, and I will inform you about what you used to do."*

To him, all of us will return. He knows what we have done, and nothing can hide away from his knowledge. Not anything will be missed, so better to be ready for that day . . .

# CHAPTER 17

# 18:58

رَبُّكَ الْغَفُورُ ذُو الرّحْمَةِ  لَوْ يُؤَاخِذُهُم بِمَا كَسَبُوا لَعَجّلَ لَهُمُ الْعَذَابَ  بَل لَهُم مَوْعِدٌ لّن يَجِدُوا مِن دُونِهِ مَوْئِلاً

*" And your Lord is the Forgiving, full of mercy. If He were to impose blame upon them for what they earned, He would have hastened for them the punishment. "*

- Here Allah says how wide the capacity for forgiveness and mercy is, and that he forgives sins and accepts those who repent to him. Allah is All-Forbearing and does not accelerate the punishment; he gives reminders to people to repent in life, to give back anything they took from others.

*" Rather, for them is an appointment from which they will never find an escape. "*

- They have their time where there is no repenting after and no escape or way out from death. Death will happen to every human, from the greatest prophet to the worst sinner. All will stand in front of Allah. The Almighty will give people time to ask for forgiveness from sin, but he does not neglect nor forget. It is a matter of time, and it is best to start before it is too late and try to do good before it is impossible.

# CHAPTER 18

# 3:135

وَالَّذِينَ إِذَا فَعَلُوا فَاحِشَةً أَوْ ظَلَمُوا أَنْفُسَهُمْ ذَكَرُوا اللَّـهَ فَاسْتَغْفَرُوا لِذُنُوبِهِمْ وَمَن يَغْفِرُ الذُّنُوبَ إِلَّا اللَّـهُ وَلَمْ يُصِرُّوا عَلَىٰ مَا فَعَلُوا وَهُمْ يَعْلَمُونَ

*" And those who, when they commit an immorality or wrong themselves [by transgression], remember Allah and seek forgiveness for their sins - and who can forgive sins except Allah? "*

- And who among us won't fall under this category of sinners! But the path we are after is seeking God's forgiveness, and only his. This verse reconfirms monotheism, as most of the Quran does because there is no one except Allah who can forgive sins; no prophet nor righteous people can. Allah is the only deity we turn to for forgiveness, and by that action, we reject any other deity.

*" and [who] do not persist in what they have done while they know."*

- One of the conditions to gain forgiveness is not insisting on wrongdoing with knowledge. Some people do sin, and they don't know it is a sin; those are excused by ignorance, as Allah is just. He won't punish until a person understands by being informed that the action he is doing is a punishable sin. But if the person knows and insists on doing it, he removes himself by his choice from God's forgiveness. And the word يصروا in Arabic links to normal strength. People can be seen who sin with the intention to sin and keep sinning with full knowledge. There is a differentiation between people who know what they do is a sin but do it due to weakness in self and seek God's forgiveness, and those who sin knowing it is a sin and insist on it without seeking forgiveness.

# CHAPTER 19

# 18:23-24

Allah says in his holy book:

وَمَا كَانَ هَٰذَا الْقُرْآنُ أَن يُفْتَرَىٰ مِن دُونِ اللَّـهِ وَلَٰكِن تَصْدِيقَ الَّذِي بَيْنَ يَدَيْهِ وَتَفْصِيلَ الْكِتَابِ لَا رَيْبَ فِيهِ مِن رَّبِّ الْعَالَمِينَ (٣٧) أَمْ يَقُولُونَ افْتَرَاهُ قُلْ فَأْتُوا بِسُورَةٍ مِّثْلِهِ وَادْعُوا مَنِ اسْتَطَعْتُم مِّن دُونِ اللَّـهِ إِن كُنتُمْ صَادِقِينَ

*" And it was not [possible] for this Qur'an to be produced by other than Allah, "*

- God confirms that there is no other source for the Quran beside him, the Almighty. The verses and chapters are without error or mistake, which is beyond human ability. It is impossible for a person who masters the language not to have an error or small mistake, yet the chapters are without grammatical or structural error, in a language that has the strictest grammar which goes up to the sound of the same letter, which is known as Tashkeel or Arabic diacritics. That is from the language point of view, which is in addition to other aspects where the Quran is above any error.

*"but [it is] a confirmation of what was before it and a detailed explanation of the [former] Scripture."*

- The Quran is the Judge and the checkpoint for any previous books if they include the truth or they were changed by Man over time. If the Quran confirms a point in other scriptures, then it did happen. If it disagrees or rejects a claim, then it didn't happen and is just human-made or not related to what was revealed to that prophet. It includes Allah's final laws to humanity, stating what is allowed, and what is forbidden, what is a good deed and what is not.

*" about which there is no doubt, from the Lord of the worlds."*

- There is no doubt in its source nor who he is, as he is Allah, Almighty, the lord of the worlds, our world we know as humans and other worlds we don't know about.

*" Or do they say [about the Prophet], "He invented it?"*

- That did happen in Mohammad's time, is happening today, and will happen tomorrow. People claim Mohammad wrote the Quran, or claim that he was a poet or an insane person and this is the result of that. There are many other claims we even hear today from many who reject the source of the Quran, and God notes that in his book.

*" Say, then bring forth a surah like it and call upon [for assistance] whomever you can besides Allah, if you should be truthful. "*

- The Almighty answers back go ahead call your friends, your top linguistic buddies , or whoever you claim that they are, your idols or spirits or whatever you want, put all your ability and capability into it, and just bring one chapter equal to the chapters of the Quran, only one in Arabic that has the same build and same strength. And that challenge was to all Arabs in that time when the Arabic language was in it is the peak, when a poet stood and improvised a 1000-line poem without a stop, as Arabs were masters of poetry with a showcase of language capabilities. God  challenges those to bring one chapter equal to the Quran chapters; the challenge is still standing to whoever can.

# 15: 95 - 99

Allah says in his holy book:

فَاصْدَعْ بِمَا تُؤْمَرُ وَأَعْرِضْ عَنِ الْمُشْرِكِينَ

إِنَّا كَفَيْنَاكَ الْمُسْتَهْزِئِينَ (95) الَّذِينَ يَجْعَلُونَ مَعَ اللَّهِ إِلَـٰهًا آخَرَ ۚ فَسَوْفَ يَعْلَمُونَ (96)

وَلَقَدْ نَعْلَمُ أَنَّكَ يَضِيقُ صَدْرُكَ بِمَا يَقُولُونَ (97) فَسَبِّحْ بِحَمْدِ رَبِّكَ وَكُن مِّنَ السَّاجِدِينَ (98)

وَاعْبُدْ رَبَّكَ حَتَّىٰ يَأْتِيَكَ الْيَقِينُ

*" Then declare what you are commanded and turn away from the polytheists. "*

- Order to Mohammad PBUH and Muslims after him: don't hide your faith. Declare Allah's words, read the Quran out loud, establish and declare Allah as one God above all, hold to Monotheism, and don't look or follow the polytheists in their claims.

*" Indeed, we are sufficient for you against the mockers."*

- Allah, he will take care of those who mock his words and make fun of his verses, so don't worry about that. They won't be able to hide God's words with their jokes and mockery.

*" Who make [equal] with Allah another deity. But they are going to know."*

- For those who make false claims about Allah, Allah will leave them in this life and give them a chance and another chance, but will they use those chances? They read and hear his words, but their desires, ego, pride, and emotions keep them from admitting that there is no God but Allah. But one day, when it is too late, they will know there is no God but Allah.

*" And We already know that your breast is constrained by what they say. "*

- God knows that their insults and claims about God are painful to Muslims; it is hard in our hearts and puts tears in the eyes of many when they hear what they claim about Allah, as we know how mighty Allah is.

*"So, exalt [Allah] with praise of your Lord and be of those who prostrate [to Him]."*

- Praise Allah, and worship him and be with whom worship him. Prostrate to him and feel his might, and what is more comforting to the heart of a believer than prostrating to God in full submission. That removes all the sadness and hard feeling from what they claim.

*" And worship your Lord until there comes to you the certainty (death)."*

- Worship Allah. Follow his religion, Islam. And hold to it; don't be taken away from it by life's challenges and hard times. Worship him until your soul departs from your body, where the journey is finished in this life, and the Judgement starts.

# CHAPTER 21

# 29:2-6

أَحَسِبَ النَّاسُ أَن يُتْرَكُوا أَن يَقُولُوا آمَنَّا وَهُمْ لاَ يُفْتَنُونَ (٢) وَلَقَدْ فَتَنَّا الَّذِينَ مِن قَبْلِهِمْ فَلَيَعْلَمَنَّ اللَّـهُ الَّذِينَ صَدَقُوا وَلَيَعْلَمَنَّ الْكَاذِبِينَ (٣) أَمْ حَسِبَ الَّذِينَ يَعْمَلُونَ السَّيِّئَاتِ أَن يَسْبِقُونَا سَاءَ مَا يَحْكُمُونَ (٤) مَن كَانَ يَرْجُو لِقَاءَ اللَّـهِ فَإِنَّ أَجَلَ اللَّـهِ لآتٍ وَهُوَ السَّمِيعُ الْعَلِيمُ (٥) وَمَن جَاهَدَ فَإِنَّمَا يُجَاهِدُ لِنَفْسِهِ إِنَّ اللَّـهَ لَغَنِيٌّ عَنِ الْعَالَمِينَ

" *Do the people think that they will be left to say, "We believe," and they will not be tried?* "

- This is the answer for those who say, "I am done with saying I believe." Saying I believe alone is just words and nothing more than a start, and it in itself is not enough. People will be tested to see who holds to faith. God will order those who don't to leave what they desire to see if this claim that they love God is true or not. For example, in Ramadan, Muslims leave food for hours to confirm the point that they believe in

God, and it is not just easy words they say. In the first moment that things get hard, do they drop it?

" *But we have certainly tried those before them, and Allah will surely make evident those who are truthful, and He will surely make evident the liars.* "

- This is nothing new in that it was done to people before. They faced hardships to confirm whether they would hold to their faith or if they were just repeating lies.

" *Or do those who do evil deeds think they can outrun us? Evil is what they judge.* "

- Do people who disbelieve or associate with God anything else think that they can escape with the bad deeds they do? And they won't be judged? That is a false thought. To God, they will return today, or after 100 years, their life will end, and then they will be judged.

*"Whoever should hope for the meeting with Allah - indeed, the term decreed by Allah is coming. And He is the Hearing, the Knowing.* "

- The believers and those who follow his words in the Quran by actions and good deeds don't have anything to worry about, so they look forward to the day they will meet Allah. Allah tells them the time is coming, and there is no chance anyone will escape the judgment day. The Almighty hears the prayers and knows what is in our hearts. He knows who prays truthfully and who prays to show off in front of people or to get fame.

*"And whoever strives only strives for [the benefit of] himself. Indeed, Allah is free from need of the worlds. (6)"*

- By following his orders. we reach happiness in life and after it. He is all-knowing. His wisdom is something we can't grasp. We follow his orders not because he needs us, but for our own benefit,         as         we         need         him.

# CHAPTER 22

# 3:59-60

Allah says in his holy book:

إنَّ مَثْلَ عِيسَىٰ عِندَ اللَّـهِ كَمَثَلِ آدَمَ ۖ خَلَقَهُ مِن تُرَابٍ ثُمَّ قَالَ لَهُ كُن فَيَكُونُ (٥٩) الْحَقُّ مِن رَّبِّكَ فَلاَ تَكُن مِّنَ الْمُمْتَرِينَ

*" Indeed, the example of Jesus to Allah is like that of Adam. He created Him from dust; then He said to him, "Be," and he was."*

-The verse includes answers to two groups, one group which rejects the virgin birth of Jesus (mainly the Jews, who question how a woman can get pregnant and give birth without a man). Allah answers that Adam was created from dust, and you as a theist believe that without a doubt, so you doubt a virgin birth?

Also, it contains an answer for Christians who claim divinity for Jesus or link him to God as his son. As the sign of the divinity of Jesus is that he was born from a human without a father, then Adam, who is created from dust, is a more significant sign and has a stronger link, as you all know Adam was created as a fully grown, adult human. He didn't pass through the stages of need and helplessness like Jesus as an infant. And he was created directly by Allah without the involvement of any other means. Jesus was created from his mother. So, both are simply a creation of God by his words "Be," and they were.

*" The truth is from your Lord, so do not be among the doubters. "*

- That is the truth from Allah in his final book, the Quran, and an answer of logic for everyone who believes in creation. Creating Adam is greater than the creation of Jesus, and no one will call Adam son of God, so Jesus logically can't be too, peace be upon them. But will people allow logic to overcome emotions? What do they grow up hearing? Their social demands? Or they will twist words and thoughts? A Muslim should have a full submission to Allah without associating anyone with him and believe that the truth is in his holy book and not in other claims.

# 49:6

Allah says in his holy book:

يَا أَيُّهَا الَّذِينَ آمَنُوا إِن جَاءَكُمْ فَاسِقٌ بِنَبَإٍ فَتَبَيَّنُوا أَن تُصِيبُوا قَوْمًا بِجَهَالَةٍ فَتُصْبِحُوا عَلَىٰ مَا فَعَلْتُمْ نَادِمِينَ

*" O you who have believed, if there comes to you a disobedient one with information, investigate,"*

- An order which we need today more than any other time, as in this sea of media and social media news, memes, videos, etc., there is a massive amount of fake news, fake claims, false information, and fabricated data. A person needs to investigate and avoid agreeing just because the story or information fits his narrative or his stereotypical idea about certain people, political parties, races, religions, or countries. A person is required to ensure that this news is factual, not only in words but in context. A person needs to Investigate and not just listen.

*" lest you harm a people out of ignorance and become, over what you have done, regretful. "*

- Today we see this spreading of false information which people neglect to confirm and news whose sources are not checked. This results in a buildup of hate and dislikes for religion or group of people. That dislike might result in racism, discrimination, or even terrorism and crime. An example is what we have seen in Christchurch, which is a result of a massive buildup of misinformation. Some people, when they recognize that they lived in an illusion, nothing like reality, are regretful, but it is too late; harm has already been done.

# 7:28-29

Allah says in his holy book:

وَإِذَا فَعَلُوا فَاحِشَةً قَالُوا وَجَدْنَا عَلَيْهَا آبَاءَنَا وَاللَّـهُ أَمَرَنَا بِهَا ۗ قُلْ إِنَّ اللَّـهَ لَا يَأْمُرُ
بِالْفَحْشَاءِ ۖ أَتَقُولُونَ عَلَى اللَّـهِ مَا لَا تَعْلَمُونَ (٢٨) قُلْ أَمَرَ رَبِّي بِالْقِسْطِ ۖ وَأَقِيمُوا وُجُوهَكُمْ
عِندَ كُلِّ مَسْجِدٍ وَادْعُوهُ مُخْلِصِينَ لَهُ الدِّينَ ۚ كَمَا بَدَأَكُمْ تَعُودُونَ

*" And when they commit an immorality, they say, "We found our fathers doing it, and Allah has ordered us to do it."*

- When people do wrong or bring a claim forward against God in a collective manner and make that claim a method to follow God, calling it faith and that wrongdoing or association with God is something they found their fathers doing and that their society does. This answer is an easy way out when you ask a group of people why they do something. You ask why they claim these things about Allah, and they will say, "oh it is our books, and we got them from our ancestors. And they don't stop there; they go further and say, "Allah ordered those actions and told us to worship or associate with him this and that." They said that to Mohammad, Peace Be Upon Him, 1400 years ago, and they say it today too.

*"Say, 'Indeed, Allah does not order immorality. Do you say about Allah that which you do not know?"*

- Here God orders us to answer back that no way does Allah order wrongdoing, nor would he will send his prophets to humanity to request them to spread wrongdoing nor to associate anyone with him. So, don't say about Allah what you don't know or link false claims you can't even confirm that those prophets said to your fathers.

*"Say, [O Muhammad], "My Lord has ordered justice and that you maintain yourselves [in worship of Him] at every place [or time] of prostration, and invoke Him, sincere to Him in religion."*

- Here Allah orders Mohammad PBUH to teach them that Allah order justice and good deeds. The Almighty doesn't order discrimination or favors of one race over all mankind, as some do claim. Allah is justice, and all humans are equal. He ordered you to be purely monotheistic, only worshipping him and praying to him in every position and time. In times of struggle and in times of ease, seek him and only him, and when you worship in the religion by praying, fasting, and doing charity, you do it sincerely to Allah and not to show off. You don't do it for some righteous person. You do it for Allah and only him.

*" Just as He originated you, you will return [to life] - "*

- As he created you, he will return you to life, even if your bones are rotten to dust, and this is a reminder that sincerity in religion and monotheism is the way forward. This is what will count in front of Allah, even if thousands of years pass and our physical bodies are rotten. He who created us from dust can bring us back again. Then we stand in front of the Almighty in a day where there is no king or slave nor white or black; we are all waiting for his mercy. Exalted is Allah above whatever they associate with Him, Sovereign of the Day of Recompense.

# 41:46

مَنْ عَمِلَ صَالِحًا فَلِنَفْسِهِ وَمَنْ أَسَاءَ فَعَلَيْهَا وَمَا رَبُّكَ بِظَلَّامٍ لِلْعَبِيدِ

*" Whoever does righteousness - it is for his [own] soul; and whoever does evil [does so] against it."*

- When you do good or follow Allah's order, you do it for your own self. It won't add anything to God, nor is he in need of it. It is a choice of your free will. The Almighty draws the path to heaven, and the rest is a path to punishment. It is your choice which path you will take. It is wrong that people assume that God needs their good deeds. You need your good deeds more than anyone else, and you need to avoid bad deeds more than anyone else because no one will be judged based on your deeds beside you.

*" And your Lord is not ever unjust to [His] servants."*

- Allah is justice, and one of his 99 names we know about is Al-Adl, which means The Just. He won't punish anyone for something he didn't do nor something he has no hand in. There is no original sin in Islam, as that is seen against Allah's justice.

God will forgive sin if he will, but in judgment day, for harm done to another person or animal, a person will be punished. For, even if God forgives another sin which might be worse, he is just and gave the abused person the right to seek justice in front of him from his abuser. That is why Muslims who understand Islam know that the worst sin is a sin against other person or animal, as it is often hard to meet that person again to say sorry or ask for forgiveness.

# CHAPTER 26

# 5:83

وَإِذَا سَمِعُوا مَا أُنزِلَ إِلَى الرَّسُولِ تَرَىٰ أَعْيُنَهُمْ تَفِيضُ مِنَ الدَّمْعِ مِمَّا عَرَفُوا مِنَ الْحَقِّ
يَقُولُونَ رَبَّنَا آمَنَّا فَاكْتُبْنَا مَعَ الشَّاهِدِينَ

*" And when they hear what has been revealed to the Messenger, you see their eyes overflowing with tears "*

- This is the effect of the words of the Quran; it touches the soul and the heart. And even when someone doesn't understand when they hear the words, tears overtake them; that is how the Quran touches the soul.

*" because of what they have recognized of the truth. "*

- They know those are not Mohammad's words or any other human's. They are the words of truth and the words of the Almighty. Those words don't have errors or mistakes.

" *They say, 'Our Lord, we have believed, so register us among the witnesses.'*"

- And this is the moment of peace, where humans drop the ego and pride, and they admit that Allah is their lord. They submit and ask Allah to count them as believers.

# 16:90

إنّ اللهَ يَأْمُرُ بِالْعَدْلِ وَالْإِحْسَانِ وَإِيتَاءِ ذِي الْقُرْبَىٰ وَيَنْهَىٰ عَنِ الْفَحْشَاءِ وَالْمُنكَرِ وَالْبَغْيِ يَعِظُكُمْ لَعَلَّكُمْ تَذَكَّرُونَ

*" Indeed, Allah orders justice and good conduct and giving to relatives"*

- A clear order from Allah to be just to others and to self, to not harm others nor harm self, to be just in talking about Allah, and to not make false claims about him nor link false idols to him, regardless of whether they are prophets or stones. He orders justice when dealing with people, which includes no cheating or lies in deals or business. And he orders good conduct or "Ihasan," and that is the highest level of good conduct, when the outside action is good but not as good as intentions, so the person intended to do more good deeds, but the surroundings limited him. That is a pure intention and pure heart. And then "giving to relatives" is mentioned, which means they could be as close as cousins or as far it can go. Helping relatives results in removing envy and building a strong society and a strong community based on love and wishing good to others.

*" and forbids immorality and bad conduct and oppression. "*

- This part includes every action Islam sees as sin and every action people see as bad conduct, including actions where it seems good from the outside, but the intention in the heart is bad. Also, Allah forbids oppression, regardless of whether it is taking people's money by force or trick, it is terrorism, or it is mass murder. Those are all huge sins that Allah the Almighty forbids.

*" He admonishes you that perhaps you will be reminded "*

- In the Quran and the teachings of the prophet PBUH, he reminds us of Allah's orders and how to follow them, telling us to hold to them to have happiness in this life and beyond and to avoid what he forbids, as it will cause only harm to us or others in this life and beyond.

# 2:204-206

وَمِنَ النّاسِ مَن يُعْجِبُكَ قَوْلُهُ فِي الْحَيَاةِ الدُّنْيَا وَيُشْهِدُ اللهَ عَلَىٰ مَا فِي قَلْبِهِ وَهُوَ أَلَدُّ الْخِصَامِ (204) وَإِذَا تَوَلَّىٰ سَعَىٰ فِي الأَرْضِ لِيُفْسِدَ فِيهَا وَيُهْلِكَ الْحَرْثَ وَالنَّسْلَ  وَاللهُ لاَ يُحِبُّ الْفَسَادَ (205) وَإِذَا قِيلَ لَهُ اتَّقِ اللهَ أَخَذَتْهُ الْعِزَّةُ بِالإِثْمِ  فَحَسْبُهُ جَهَنَّمُ  وَلَبِئْسَ الْمِهَادُ

*" And of the people is he whose speech pleases you in worldly life, and he calls Allah to witness as to what is in his heart "*

- The kind of people who speak with great confidence and well-mannered speech. When they talk, they amaze others. Their words are well chosen. People are attracted to listening to them and feel pleased by their words, as they are reflections of the heart.

*"yet he is the fiercest of opponents."*

- When you start debating, asking questions to confirm, or discussing the matter, this person changes it to a personal attack or uses aggression as a defense. The believer takes things with ease and won't feel the need for aggression, as his words—even if they are not sugarcoated—are based on truth, and he who holds truth is not bothered nor insulted if asked to prove it. The aim of a believer's speech is simply to show the truth, not like the person described in this verse.

" *And when he goes away, he strives throughout the land to cause corruption therein and destroy crops and animals. And Allah does not like corruption.* "

- Here the verse talks about how their actions don't fit their calls of rightness, as they spread harm and corruption against every living thing. This verse clearly fits the actions done by terrorist groups. They try to sugarcoat their call by using words which have an emotional effect and using lies under the guise of truth. But they act by terror and hate, without respect to the religion they claim to follow. Allah dislikes corruption and therefore dislikes them.

" And when it is said to him, "Fear Allah," pride in the sin takes hold of him. Sufficient for him is Hellfire, and how wretched is the resting place. "

- When scholars and people of knowledge advise them to stop those actions of terror and "Fear Allah," they get blinded by their ego and hold strongly to their sins, ignoring all others. From the beginning, they have been using lies and sugarcoated words. They didn't have the heart of a believer; they had the heart of a hypocrite. That is why Allah will punish them in Hell due to what they have done. They never listened to advice, and they waged war on Allah the Almighty and the prophet PBUH by spreading terror and giving a bad image to Islam, Allah's final religion, which the Almighty sent to all mankind. They will not just enter Hell for some time; they will stay in it forever.

# CHAPTER 29

# 21:35

كُلُّ نَفْسٍ ذَائِقَةُ الْمَوْتِ وَنَبْلُوكُم بِالشَّرِّ وَالْخَيْرِ فِتْنَةً وَإِلَيْنَا تُرْجَعُونَ

*" Every soul will taste death. "*

- That every Human soul will leave its body one day, as death is a transition from the world, we know to a new domain. The soul doesn't die; the body dies. A soul leaves the body and every beloved one behind. There is great pain when the soul leaves whom it knows and goes to a place it doesn't know. Our soul might feel what is around but can't command that dead, cold body anymore. That is the point of no return, where no repenting nor belief will help. It is the moment where there is no other chance. We had enough chances in life, and we had the will to choose between what is true and what is false, between desires and clear truth, between the words of God and the words of people. The challenge is that we don't know when that moment will happen. Someone might jump off a building trying to kill himself but live for 10 more years, and a person just walking along might drop dead . . . so, are we ready?

*" And We test you with evil and with good as trial; "*

- Here is our life, full of joy and pain as a trial. If we have joy, will we thank God ? Will the rich feed the poor? Will we worship God more if we are healthy while others are sick? People think bad things are tests to see how they hold up the belief in God. but for me, good things are harder. In bad times you don't have much of choices, but in good times, you have lots of choices. If you are rich, you can eat for 10 to 100 dollars a meal or spend 1000 dollars to feed desires and fantasies, but when you are poor, you don't have a choice beside hunger. If evil happened to us, would it make us doubt Allah? Blame him? Ignore faith? Seek refuge in temporary happiness? Or will we hold up and keep faith strong in One God, and even avoid any false claim to just worship Allah, without a son, without a spouse, without equal, and without medium—just purely Allah. Or would we seek idols and figures? Anything besides following and worshipping Allah as he ordered is just the illusion of a dreamer.

*"and to Us you will be returned. "*

- That is the fact, without a doubt. We will return to Allah and only him. He knows what good we did to show off and what good we did purely to worship him. He knows if we sin, even if we try to hide it from all people. Nothing is hidden from him, so to          him,          we          will          return.

# 49:13

يَا أَيُّهَا النَّاسُ إِنَّا خَلَقْنَاكُم مِّن ذَكَرٍ وَأُنثَىٰ وَجَعَلْنَاكُمْ شُعُوبًا وَقَبَائِلَ لِتَعَارَفُوا ۚ إِنَّ أَكْرَمَكُمْ عِندَ اللَّـهِ أَتْقَاكُمْ ۚ إِنَّ اللَّـهَ عَلِيمٌ خَبِيرٌ

*" O mankind, indeed, we have created you from male and female."*

-The verse starts with stating the international approach of Islam to mankind. It is not limited to a group or generation, nor is it limited to a time or location. The verse starts with "O mankind" as a call for every human, stating a fact in Islam that all of  us are created from male and female, regardless of our skin color, height, gender, or other factors and characteristics used to divide us. We are all equal from one source. There is no superiority between us. We are all God's creatures. Islam is against any call of discrimination based on race.

*" and made you peoples and tribes that you may know one another."*

-   And he made us into tribes and groups, and our differences are due to our environment or other factors, but that should not stop us from knowing each other and mixing with each other, because all of us came from the same source.

*" Indeed, the most noble of you in the sight of Allah is the most righteous of you. "*

- And the only difference between us, which counts in front of God is being more righteous in following religion and having the purest monotheistic belief in God.

" Indeed, Allah is Knowing and Acquainted. "

- And that level of righteousness is only known to Allah; he knows who is the most righteous among us. I might say I am good, but my say is just words; God knows what is in my heart, and no one else can know that, so this hidden characteristic can't be used between us to discriminate. That is why Islam is anti-discrimination, as the sole criteria of superiority between us can only be confirmed by God.

# The End

As the month of Ramadan, this year is 29 days and finished on the 3rd of June, I stop here and hope that I continue with this next year inshallah. And I hope you enjoyed reading this short book.

Printed in Great Britain
by Amazon